Documents of American Democracy

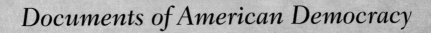

EMANCIPATION PROCLAMATION

Ryan Nagelhout

PowerKiDS
press.

New York

Published in 2017 by The Rosen Publishing Group, Inc.
29 East 21st Street, New York, NY 10010

Editor: Katie Kawa
Book Design: Tanya Dellaccio

Photo Credits: Cover (painting), pp. 5 (Lincoln), 8, 17 (painting) Everett Historical/Shutterstock.com; cover (document), pp. 5, 27 Courtesy of the National Archives; Background (all pages except 19) didecs/Shutterstock.com; p. 7 (top) sjgh/Shutterstock.com; pp. 7 (bottom),11 (document), 13, 17 (document), 19, 21 Courtesy of the Library of Congress; p. 9 https://commons.wikimedia.org/wiki/File:Ordinance_of_Secession_Milledgeville,_Georgia_1861.png; p. 11 (painting) MPI/Getty Images; pp. 15, 23 Buyenlarge/Getty Images; p. 25 DEA/W.BUSS/Getty Images; p. 29 https://commons.wikimedia.org/wiki/File:AdoptionOf13thAmendment.jpg.

Library of Congress Cataloging-in-Publication Data

Names: Nagelhout, Ryan, author.
Title: Emancipation Proclamation / Ryan Nagelhout.
Description: New York : PowerKids Press, [2016] | Series: Documents of
   American democracy | Includes index.
Identifiers: LCCN 2016011091 | ISBN 9781499420814 (pbk.) | ISBN 9781499420838 (library bound) | ISBN 9781499420821 (6 pack)
Subjects: LCSH: United States. President (1861-1865 : Lincoln). Emancipation
   Proclamation–Juvenile literature. | Lincoln, Abraham, 1809-1865–Juvenile
   literature. | Slaves–Emancipation–United States–Juvenile literature. |
   United States–Politics and government–1861-1865–Juvenile literature.
Classification: LCC E453 .N54 2016 | DDC 973.7/14–dc23
LC record available at http://lccn.loc.gov/2016011091

Manufactured in the United States of America

CPSIA Compliance Information: Batch #BS16PK: For Further Information contact Rosen Publishing, New York, New York at 1-800-237-9932

CONTENTS

Certain things can be lost to history. Over time, ideas can become unclear, and words may lose their meaning. This is why historical documents are so valuable. These primary sources allow us to see firsthand the words and sentences that changed the world.

The Emancipation Proclamation is one of these valuable historical documents. It was written and delivered by President Abraham Lincoln during the American Civil War. Its intention was to free slaves in the states that had broken away from the Union at the start of the war. Used both as a military tool and a statement of the war's purpose, the Emancipation Proclamation marked the beginning of the end of slavery in America. It also made it clear that the Civil War wasn't simply about states' rights—it was about slavery.

*The Emancipation Proclamation is one of the most important documents in American history. However, the original **draft** of this document, which was written by Lincoln himself, was destroyed in a fire. What remains is this official copy, which was signed by Lincoln on January 1, 1863.*

Emancipation
Proclamation

Abraham Lincoln

SLAVERY IN THE SOUTH

Debates about slavery had been dividing the United States for years before the American Civil War. Southern states used slaves to keep their plantations running, while most Northern states had outlawed slavery by 1804. As the nation grew, certain territories in the West were added to the Union as states, and certain states were allowed to decide if they would allow slavery. These decisions created many conflicts.

A group of Southern states threatened to secede from, or leave, the Union if the antislavery Republican Party won the presidential election of 1860. By the time Republican Abraham Lincoln took office on March 4, 1861, seven states had left the Union. Eventually, a total of 11 states seceded and formed their own nation, which was called the Confederate States of America.

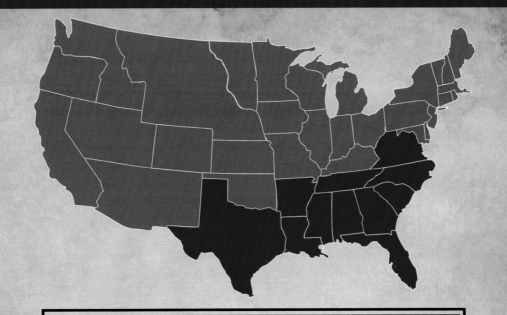

This is a map of the United States in 1861. The 11 states in red seceded and became the Confederate States of America, or Confederacy, during the Civil War.

Washington, D.C., on March 4, 1861

After the Civil War ended and as opinions about slavery have changed, some Americans—and even some historians—have claimed the Civil War wasn't fought over slavery. Instead, they claim the war was about protecting the rights of individual states against the federal government. This view, however, ignores the words of those in the South during the time of secession. Countless newspapers, politicians, and slave owners in Southern states spoke of secession as a means to protect slavery.

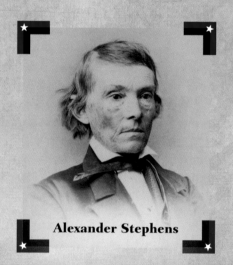

Alexander Stephens

In March 1861, the Confederacy's vice president,

★ ★ ★ ★ ★ ★ ★ ★ ★ ★ ★ ★ ★ ★ ★ ★ ★ ★

THE "PECULIAR INSTITUTION"

When the Southern states seceded from the Union, many of their formal secession documents clearly stated the most important reason they were breaking away was to protect the institution of slavery. Some secession documents refer to their "peculiar institution" of slavery. At that time, "peculiar institution" meant something that was special to them. Slavery was so important to the South—both economically and socially—that people who lived there were willing to fight and die to protect it.

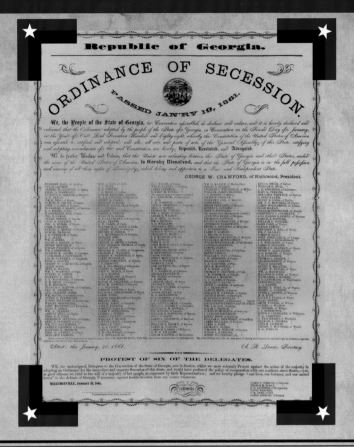

Shown here is a copy of the ordinance of secession—the document that formally announced a state's secession— voted on in Georgia. Each state in the Confederacy voted on its own ordinance of secession.

Alexander Stephens, said its government was founded on the fact that white people were superior to black people. He continued, "…its cornerstone rests upon the great truth, that the [black man] is not equal to the white man; that slavery—**subordination** to the superior race—is his natural and normal condition."

THE WAR BEGINS

On April 12, 1861, Confederate troops under General Pierre Gustav Toutant Beauregard opened fire on Fort Sumter, which was a Union fort in Charleston, South Carolina. For 34 hours, Confederate troops fired their weapons at the fort. Poorly supplied and outnumbered, the Union troops gave up the fort on April 13.

On April 15, Lincoln issued a proclamation. He called for 75,000 volunteer soldiers to join the American army to put down the Southern **insurrection**. This proclamation helped push the final four slave states to secede in the following weeks. Lincoln's presidency was only weeks old, and the country had been split in two. Lincoln later asked for more than 43,000 additional volunteers to serve in the army for three years. The American Civil War had begun, and Lincoln knew the Union needed to be prepared.

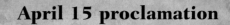

There were no official deaths during the attack on Fort Sumter, shown here. However, Lincoln knew he would need a large army to fight what was sure to be a deadly conflict. That was why he issued his proclamation on April 15, 1861.

LINCOLN'S STANCE

Although he was a member of a political party that had become known for its antislavery views, Lincoln didn't write and deliver the Emancipation Proclamation at the beginning of the Civil War. The president's intentions at the beginning of the war were clear. All he wanted was to preserve the Union by winning the war and readmitting the 11 states that had seceded.

"My **paramount** object in this struggle is to save the Union, and is not either to save or destroy Slavery," Lincoln wrote in a letter to Horace Greeley on August 22, 1862.

★ ★ ★ ★ ★ ★ ★ ★ ★ ★ ★ ★ ★ ★ ★ ★

"A HOUSE DIVIDED"

Although he didn't directly call for the end of slavery in the early days of his presidency, Lincoln was aware of its political importance. In a famous speech delivered in Springfield, Illinois, on June 16, 1858, he said, " 'A house divided against itself cannot stand.' I believe this government cannot endure, permanently, half slave and half free…. It will become all one thing or all the other." While Lincoln spoke about the issue of slavery, he didn't act to end it in any way until he knew his actions would be supported by most of the country.

Later in the letter, Lincoln stated, "What I do about Slavery…I do because I believe it helps to save this Union…." Lincoln, however, knew saving the Union meant he would eventually have to do one of two things: allow all states to have slaves or abolish slavery in every state.

URGING LINCOLN TO ACT

Lincoln's presidency was defined by the Civil War and the issue of slavery. Abolitionists, or people who wanted to end slavery, urged Lincoln to act throughout his presidency. **Radical Republicans** also pushed Lincoln to speak against slavery. However, Lincoln—trying to preserve the Union—felt he needed to keep the border states that allowed slavery from seceding. Some people living in those states had already headed south to join the Confederate army.

Congress began taking measures into its own hands to free slaves in the states that had seceded. It passed the Confiscation Acts, which allowed the Union to confiscate, or take, Confederate property. The first Confiscation Act, which was passed on August 6, 1861, also freed any slave who fought with or worked with the Confederate military.

THE SECOND CONFISCATION ACT

*The second Confiscation Act was passed on July 17, 1862. It was essentially the **precursor** to Lincoln's Emancipation Proclamation. The act states slaves of both military and nonmilitary officials in the Confederacy "shall be forever free," but it could only be enforced in Confederate lands occupied by the Union army. This language is very similar to the language Lincoln would later use in his famous proclamation.*

This painting shows a meeting between Lincoln and the famous abolitionist Frederick Douglass during the Civil War.

THE PRELIMINARY PROCLAMATION

The passing of the Confiscation Acts gave Lincoln the sense of support he needed to make his own **ultimatum** to the seceded states: End the war and rejoin the Union, or lose slavery for good. Lincoln wrote what became known as the **preliminary** Emancipation Proclamation. He showed this proclamation to two of his secretaries—William H. Seward and Gideon Welles—on July 13, 1862. On July 22, Lincoln told his cabinet about the proclamation. While not everyone was excited about it, his secretary of war—Edwin M. Stanton—wanted it announced as soon as possible.

During a cabinet meeting on September 22, 1862, some changes were made to what became the Emancipation Proclamation. Lincoln stated that day that the Emancipation Proclamation would take effect on January 1, 1863.

This copy of a print from 1866 shows Lincoln reading the preliminary Emancipation Proclamation to his cabinet.

The Emancipation Proclamation starts with a simple noting of the date: "on the twenty-second day of September, in the year of our Lord one thousand eight hundred and sixty two...." The document warns that if the South doesn't end its "**rebellion**" within 100 days—by January 1, 1863—the Emancipation Proclamation will go into effect.

The second paragraph of the proclamation was—at the time—the most important set of words in the history of the abolitionist movement in the United States. It promises, "All persons held as slaves within any State or designated part of a State...in rebellion against the United States, shall be... forever free." These words clearly state that any slave in a state that seceded from the Union would be considered free.

This is a photographed copy of the original draft of the Emancipation Proclamation. The handwriting belongs to Lincoln, and the middle section was taken from a printing of the preliminary Emancipation Proclamation.

By the President of the United States of America:

A Proclamation.

Lincoln's handwriting

Whereas, on the twentysecond day of September, in the year of our Lord one thousand eight hundred and sixtytwo, a proclamation was issued by the President of the United States, containing, among other things, the following, town:

date: September 22, 1862

That on the first day of January, in the year of our Lord one thousand eight hundred and sixty-three, all persons held as slaves within any State or designated part of a State, the people whereof shall then be in rebellion against the United States, shall be then, thenceforward, and forever free; and the Executive Government of the United States, including the military and naval authority thereof, will recognize and maintain the freedom of such persons, and will do no act or acts to repress such persons, or any of them, in any efforts they may make for their actual freedom.

That the Executive will, on the first day of January aforesaid, by proclamation, designate the States and parts of States, if any, in which the people thereof, respectively, shall then be in rebellion against the United States; and the fact that any State, or the people thereof, shall on that day be, in good faith, represented in the Congress of the United States by members chosen thereto at elections wherein a majority of the qualified voters of such State shall have participated, shall, in the absence of strong countervailing testimony, be deemed conclusive evidence that such State, and the people thereof, are not then in rebellion against the United States.

printed part of September proclamation

Now, therefore I, Abraham Lincoln, President of the United States, by virtue of the power in me vested as Commander-in-Chief, of the Army and Navy of the United States, in time of actual armed rebellion against authority and government of the United States, and as a fit and necessary war measure for suppressing said rebellion, do, on this first day of January, in the year of our Lord one thousand eight hundred and sixtythree, and in accordance with my purpose so to do, publicly proclaimed for the full period of one hundred days, from the day first above mentioned, order and designate

date the proclamation would take effect: January 1, 1863

claiming power as commander in chief during time of war

Lincoln's handwriting

20 20

19

In the second paragraph of the Emancipation Proclamation, it's also written that "the United States…will recognize and maintain the freedom of such persons, and will do no act or acts to repress such persons, or any of them, in any efforts they may make for their actual freedom." In other words, not only were slaves in Confederate states "forever free," they would be protected by the U.S. government against the Confederacy or any other group attempting to force them back into slavery.

Some abolitionists felt the Emancipation Proclamation didn't use strong enough language and didn't do enough to free slaves in border states or elsewhere. However, the Emancipation Proclamation is clear about slaves owned by Confederates. They were free, and they wouldn't have to go back to a life of slavery after the war.

The Emancipation Proclamation states that the millions of slaves in most Confederate lands were freed. However, historians believe about 750,000 slaves in the United States weren't freed by this document.

What the Emancipation Proclamation did do:	What the Emancipation Proclamation didn't do:
free slaves in states that seceded from the Union	*end slavery in America*
allow African Americans to join the Union army	*free slaves in border states and in certain areas under Union control*

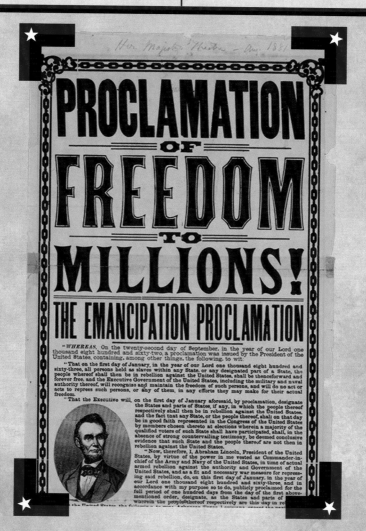

In the proclamation's fourth paragraph, Lincoln **invokes** his power as commander in chief of America's military in the "time of actual armed rebellion against the authority and government of the United States." Lincoln states that he gave the members of the Confederacy time to end the insurrection, but they continued to rebel. The document then lists the states affected by this proclamation, which are all the Confederate states.

One of the reasons Lincoln's secretary of war wanted the Emancipation Proclamation announced as soon as possible is that he realized its importance to the Union's war effort. The Emancipation Proclamation weakened the Confederacy by taking away its source of free labor. It also allowed former slaves to join the Union army.

> *By the end of the war, black soldiers made up 10 percent of Union troops.*

THEY CAN DECIDE

Later in the Emancipation Proclamation, Lincoln states, "I hereby **enjoin** upon the people so declared to be free to **abstain** from all violence, unless in necessary self-defense." Historians believe this was included to discourage freed slaves from rioting, or creating violent public disturbances. Instead, Lincoln states they should begin working for "reasonable" pay. The next paragraph, however, encourages any slaves who want to fight the Confederacy to join the Union army.

"And I further declare and make known, that such persons of suitable condition, will be received into the armed service of the United States to garrison forts, positions, stations, and other places, and to man vessels of all sorts in said service."

EXCEPTIONS TO EMANCIPATION

Lincoln made it clear that slaves in areas controlled by the Confederacy were free, but part of the Emancipation Proclamation deals with exceptions to this new rule. Most of these exceptions describe the parts of Confederate states under Union control. This meant any slaves in these areas weren't officially freed.

Twelve parishes, which are like counties, in Louisiana are named as exceptions to the Emancipation Proclamation. The document also mentions the 48 counties of Virginia that didn't secede from the Union. These counties belonged to what would become the state of West Virginia. Seven counties in Virginia that were controlled by the Union army are also named as exceptions in the Emancipation Proclamation. These areas—including the cities of Norfolk and Portsmouth—were to be "left precisely as if this proclamation were not issued."

Historians believe Lincoln included these exceptions because he was afraid the document wouldn't hold up in the Supreme Court if it wasn't clearly referring to slaves only in Confederate lands. Lincoln felt he didn't have the authority yet to declare other slaves free. He also avoided referring to slaves in Tennessee, which had seceded but was mostly under Union control by 1863.

Louisiana slave market

"Arkansas, Texas, Louisiana, (except the Parishes of St. Bernard, Plaquemines, Jefferson, St. John, St. Charles, St. James Ascension, Assumption, Terrebonne, Lafourche, St. Mary, St. Martin, and Orleans, including the City of New Orleans) Mississippi, Alabama, Florida, Georgia, South Carolina, North Carolina, and Virginia, (except the forty-eight counties designated as West Virginia, and also the counties of Berkley, Accomac, Northampton, Elizabeth City, York, Princess Ann, and Norfolk, including the cities of Norfolk and Portsmouth[)], and which excepted parts, are for the present, left precisely as if this proclamation were not issued."

THE SCRIBE'S ERROR

Lincoln's handwritten copy of the Emancipation Proclamation wasn't used as the final version. Instead, the final version arrived on Lincoln's desk on January 1, 1863, after being **engrossed** by a government scribe. As Lincoln read the engrossed document, he noticed an error. Near the end of the document, it was written, "in testimony whereof, I have hereunto set my name." This was the language used in treaties. As an executive order, the Emancipation Proclamation needed to state, "in witness whereof, I have hereunto set my hand."

THE CHICAGO FIRE

In the fall of 1863, Lincoln sent his handwritten copy of the Emancipation Proclamation to a group of women in Chicago, Illinois, who were raising money for injured Civil War soldiers. On October 8, 1871, a massive fire began burning in Chicago. It lasted for two days, killed about 300 people, and burned thousands of buildings. It also destroyed the original copy of the Emancipation Proclamation that was handwritten by Lincoln.

While a scribe rewrote the document, Lincoln hosted a number of people in honor of New Year's Day. He shook so many hands that his own hands were weak and shaky. He was worried his signature would be too shaky and would look like he was unsure of himself.

Abraham Lincoln's signature

Shown here is the final page of the engrossed version of the Emancipation Proclamation that was signed by Lincoln.

THE PROMISE OF FREEDOM

After more than four years of bloody battles, the Confederacy surrendered, and the American Civil War ended on June 2, 1865. Lincoln wouldn't live to see the war's end or the emancipation of all slaves in the United States. He was shot on April 14, 1865, while watching a play in Washington, D.C. He died the next morning.

The Emancipation Proclamation paved the way for the 13th Amendment to the U.S. Constitution, which officially outlawed slavery in the United States on December 6, 1865. The 14th and 15th Amendments granted freed slaves citizenship and the right to vote. While civil rights for African Americans were still limited by some laws and practices for decades, other laws—including the Civil Rights Act of 1964—aimed to keep Lincoln's promise of freedom.

While many were critical of the limited scale of Lincoln's Emancipation Proclamation, it laid the groundwork for many future laws granting rights to African Americans, especially the 13th Amendment. A celebration after the passage of this amendment is shown here.

"FOREVER FREE"

The time of legal slavery is a shameful period of American history many would like to forget. However, it's important to remember the horrors of slavery and how it was stopped. Abraham Lincoln's Emancipation Proclamation didn't erase slavery from our history, but it marked an important step in the journey toward freedom for all Americans. It also allowed almost 200,000 former slaves to fight for the Union and help win the war against the Confederacy.

Studying the words of the Emancipation Proclamation and the actions of President Lincoln is an important way to remember how far our nation has come. The words of this document should also inspire us to protect our fellow Americans and their right to be "forever free" in the future.

GLOSSARY

abstain: To keep from doing something.

draft: A piece of writing.

engross: To prepare the final text of an official document with larger, clearer text.

enjoin: To direct or demand.

insurrection: A fight against a group in charge.

invoke: To appeal to as an authority.

paramount: More important than other things.

precursor: Something that comes before something else.

preliminary: Coming before the main part or item.

Radical Republican: A member of the branch of the Republican Party from the Civil War era that was made up of people who were completely opposed to slavery and wanted to grant equal rights to freed slaves.

rebellion: Open fighting against authority.

subordination: The act of being placed in a lower class under the control of an authority.

ultimatum: A demand that, if ignored, could lead to forced action.

INDEX

WEBSITES

Due to the changing nature of Internet links, PowerKids Press has
developed an online list of websites related to the subject of this book.
This site is updated regularly. Please use this link to access the list:
www.powerkidslinks.com/amdoc/emproc